This book was written for the broken and those who crave healing. For the simple, the complicated, and everything in between. For those who chose love, even when love didn't choose them.

To the ones that hurt you, this is both an apology and a goodbye.

These poems are here to hold *you*.

**For The Hands That Hold Me**

I want to be the sad movie you
repeatedly watch, even when you
know the outcome, but you want
your heart to let out all the tears it
doesn't do so well with.

I want to be the book you
reread and highlight
all the words that stand out.

I want to be the bookmark in
the crucial chapters of your life.

I want to be the song that makes you cry.
The one you lay in bed with
and let the lyrics take over you.

I want to be your most cherished memory,
the one you wish to relive every second of
every day.

I want to be your fear. A fear you will soon
outgrow because the world has shown you
other things to be frightened about.

*If you think my poems are about you, they are.*

-M.A.

I want to be the poetry that grows in you and
kicks your stomach with every word you read,
thinking it's about you.

I want to be the light in your eyes
when the sorrow takes over, and you've
given up on hope.

I want to be your re-tweet on Twitter,
your shout-out on Instagram,
and your Facebook reminders.

Let me be your favorite poem,
the metaphor you could feel
without me even touching you.

# CONTENTS

Heartache     11

Heartless     81

Heartful     105

# Heartache

**Contaminated**

I remember our smiles; they
tainted our apartment walls.

**Daydreaming**

There are thoughts of you lingering.
The scent of you on my thighs visits me
and hugs the image of you in my mind.

While I prepare myself to miss you,
I see the stains of you on my bedsheets.

I can taste you on my lips as your smile
plays like a song on repeat.

### Silence Speaks Volumes

I tried

           begging you to stay

                          *with my voice,*

but you never listened,

So I tried to beg you to stay

*with my silence.*

## **Exhale**

My fingertips are catching their breath
after running up and down your spine.

## Rainbows

I never liked the color yellow
or any color that wasn't pink.
Until I met you, and your favorite
color were all the colors.

Often beauty can be seen
anywhere; you just have to be looking.
You said it was your favorite color
because it was me.

You said rainbows are what you
see, when you look at me on a bright
summer morning.

You said, sometimes when you
stare at the sky and then back at me,
you would taste all the colors in your
mouth, and I would laugh because
it never made sense to me.

I never understood how someone's
favorite color could be all the colors.

How could someone see all the
colors when they look at you?

How can they taste you
without ever tasting you?

I never understood you much,
and I guess this is why it never
worked. I liked pink, simple.

You liked all the colors of
the rainbow because you enjoy
the beauty in everything.
I just wanted pink.

The color of your lips.
That shade, was my favorite.
But you seemed to find your
favorite shade on other women's
lips.

Blue.
Blue became my
favorite color
after you left me.

## Hungry

You feed me lies
the way you feed baby food,
to a child.

### Hypocrite

I knew I loved you
when I tried to convince
myself to hate you.

## Party of Two

I'm showing up late if
you invite me over for dinner
to a party you and I
both know the actual intentions of,
so that you could feast and dance
with my heart.

**Mixed Signals**

I blame my ears for listening to your words
and trying to find love in them.

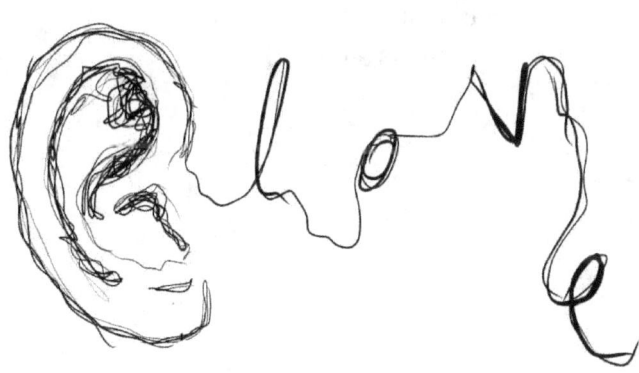

**Void**

The day you left
wasn't a day I remember
It was a day I felt.

**Cling**

You were like sand.
and no matter how much I gripped onto you,
you managed to slip away.

## Birds Trapped In Cages Pt. 1

This is

what

loving you

feels like.

**Pretty Bird**

You will soon realize you aren't scared
of the unknown. You're afraid of
starting over, so you settle for crumbs.
Broken clocks, and shitty men who
promise nothing but tight cages.
Cages that stop you from seeing
your beautiful wings.

## Birds Trapped In Cages Pt. 2

You let things slide in front of you and, as they rise and grow wings, from the cages you trapped them in, you become comfortable in toxic places looking for a new home.

**Lost**

I looked for you,
where you told me to look,
if I ever got lost,
Your absence greeted me.

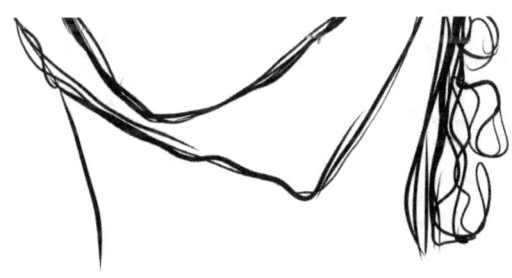

## Invisible

My eyes were yelling for you;
they wanted you to see me

*Why can't you see me?*

## With Love

You loved when my poems were about you,
but you never really knew what to tell me.
One night I convinced you to do the same for me,
and you sent it to me three days later.
You wrote about how my eyes made you feel when
you looked at them. You told me how it would feel if
I left you and how you couldn't imagine what you
would do without me.

What are you doing now?

How's life *without* me?

**Drown**

The waves inside me will drown you.
They will take you to places
you haven't seen before.

They've been hiding
inside black holes and slow tides.
They've tried to camouflage
behind closed doors and decorated
smiles.

You came along,
and with one kiss, you set them free.
The waves began to dance.

**Bittersweet**

I remember what your love tastes like,
still can't get that taste out of my mouth.

**Goodbye**

~~You never know what you have until it's gone~~
You knew what you had,
You just never thought it'd leave.

## Hanging By A Thread

If I ever expressed how I felt inside, I think your insides would shatter, and even then, you'd still use those pieces to slice me open.

**Floating**

Time flies, and my time with you
grew a pair of wings

and left.

## What Love Shouldn't Feel Like

I've been picking at the scabs created
from the last time I fell in love.

## When He Isn't The One

When he isn't the one, you sleep
next to him with your arms open.
You learn what one-way hugs
feel like and how his warmth isn't
enough to heat the feelings inside you.

You grow love for them in
the most innocent way, and when
you're apart, you do get sad. You
may even miss them, and for the
slightest second, you try to convince
yourself that maybe you are falling
for him.

He may even make you cry
make you feel some pain, and
although it stings and it catches you
by surprise, you've felt pain before,
and this, this just isn't it.

You may rest next to him, but
your mind is always wondering,
his eyes may glisten when
seeing your face in the morning,
but yours, they, they cry out for things
you can't find in him.

You stay.

You don't know why you stay or
why you can't simply tell him
your I love you's don't have his name.
You see the amount of hurt that'll cause.
You've been there before, so you stay.
After all that time, you finally realize you
shouldn't have stayed, so you leave.

## Aching

Loving you is like eating ice cream
with your two front teeth missing

## Tomatoes

You had tomato-tasting kisses laying on your
forehead, that afternoon before you left.
I remember because I tasted like ketchup,
you taught me.

## Yearning

I'm up every night
replaying your smile
in my mind
and I don't know which one
I miss more,
*yours or mine.*

## Splinters

Tell me when you decided it was
safe enough to hand over your heart
to someone who has hands full of splinters.
Tell me about the first time you
revealed your love to someone
without using words.

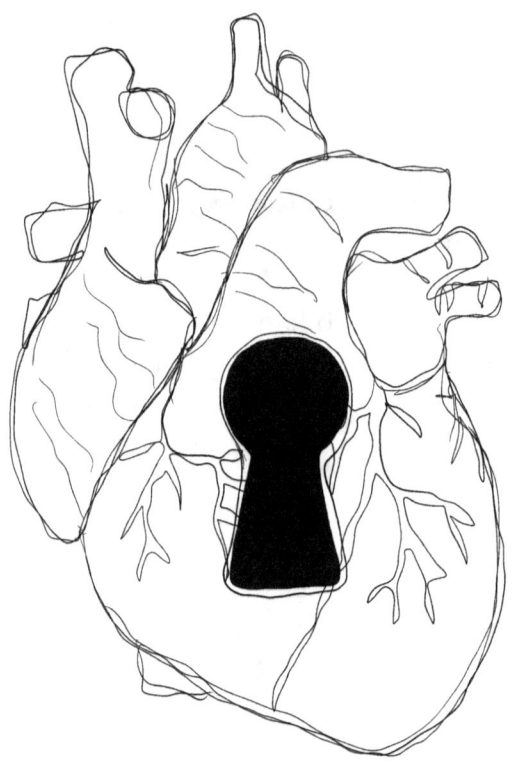

**Abandoned**

I have this empty hole in my heart. I got it from loving you so much pieces within me started to disintegrate.

**Shared Lips**

I can find out what I need to know from your kisses;
I can read them like my favorite bedtime story.

**Master Piece**

You want me partially,
and I'm not sure
you could have
only a fraction of what I am.

**Self-destruction**

We picked ourselves apart;
*flowers without petals.*

## Yin And Yang

I sometimes wonder,
what things have happened
in my life that make me feel this way?
Some days I want to feel nothing,
and some days
I'd kill to feel *alive.*

**Ticking Clock**

I wanted to be like time, numb.
No matter what, it always moves on.

## The Aftermath

I kept digging my tongue in you,
even after I knew the consequences
of living with a crooked smile.

**Runaway**

I copied the feelings you left behind
and pasted them onto newer memories,
in case you ever came back.

## The Day Our Souls Kissed

Do you remember
when I made you smile?
It was the day our souls
connected in a way
we couldn't describe.

Do you remember the vibes?

Do you remember our hearts
telling us we've met before?

**Karma**

I crave you despite all the hurt you've caused me.

**Toxic**

I tried leaving you, I really did.

**Surrender**

The fear of losing you,
pleaded with me

until I gave in.

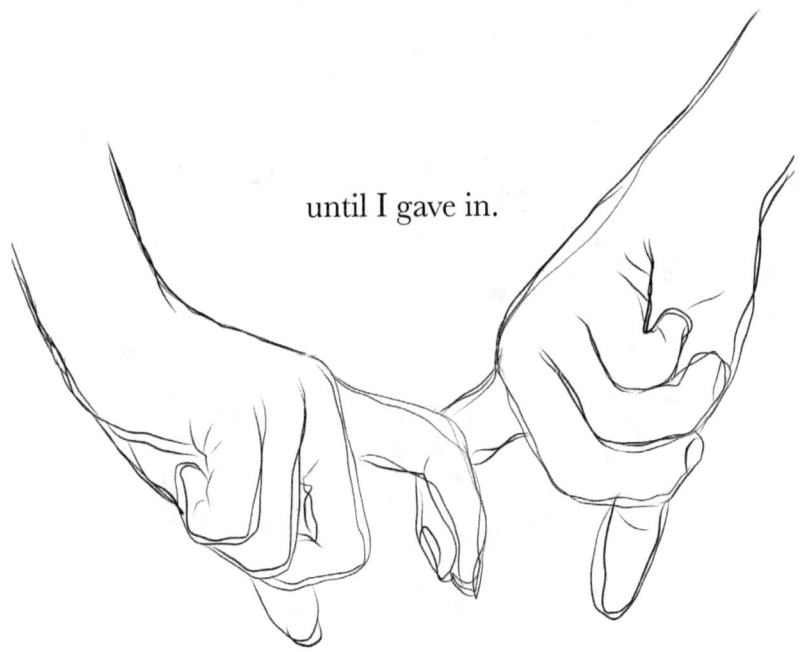

## **Relapse**

I think of you like run-on sentences.

**Blurred Vision**

Happiness is just an illusion,
pictures taken
off of broken cameras.

## **Farewell**

I am standing in the desert with a
fork in my hand, scrapping off the
parts of me you stayed with,
collecting my things,
ready to move on.

### I Found Your Pieces In Another Person's Bed

My head felt the coldness
of your empty shoulders,
my hands the abandonment of yours,
my heart missed the speed bumps
it used to run over,
trying to catch up to yours.

## Sweet & Sour

I know that there are nights
where you don't think of me.
Nights where my name or
our memories do not cross
your mind.

I know that some days
you sleep peacefully,
and your heartaches
don't wake you.

I know that many times
when you lay with someone else,
you lay with someone else,
and don't see them as my
replacement.

Frequently, you don't think of
my well-being. You don't read
my poems and try to figure out
if I write them for you.

I know that your lips often
become tired and that
my lips aren't the ones
who put them to rest.

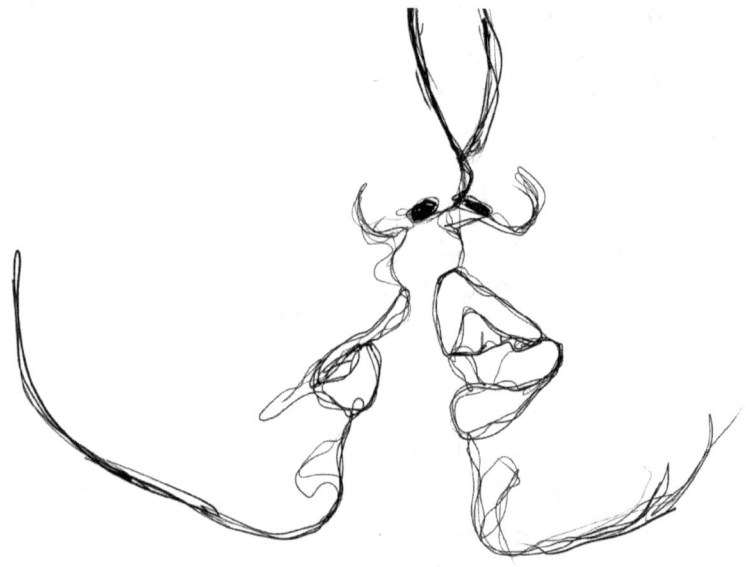

## Souls

I've loved you sometime before,
maybe when we were both
nothing but two souls;
*this feels like deja vu.*

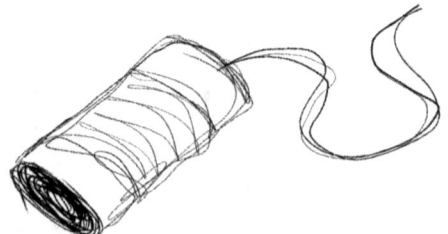

### Hello?

It's like we're both yelling
through disconnected phones.

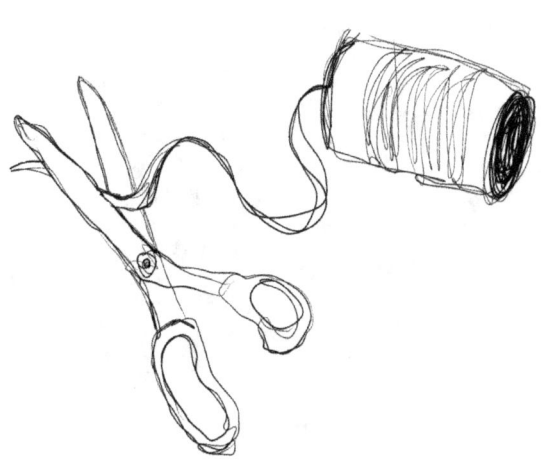

**Depart**

I want to buy a one-way ticket to your heart
and run away with you.

## Equal Exchange

I'm giving you my heart
hoping that I get one in return.

### He Loves Me, He Loves Me Not

When I said *"I love you,"*
you replied *"I don't know."*

## Ego

I am here to show you what you deserve,
but that doesn't mean I'll be the one to give it to
you.

## Lessons Learned The Hard Way

You never love the same way twice;
the second time you're more cautious.

## Trapped

You don't love me. You just can't see me be happy *with someone else.*

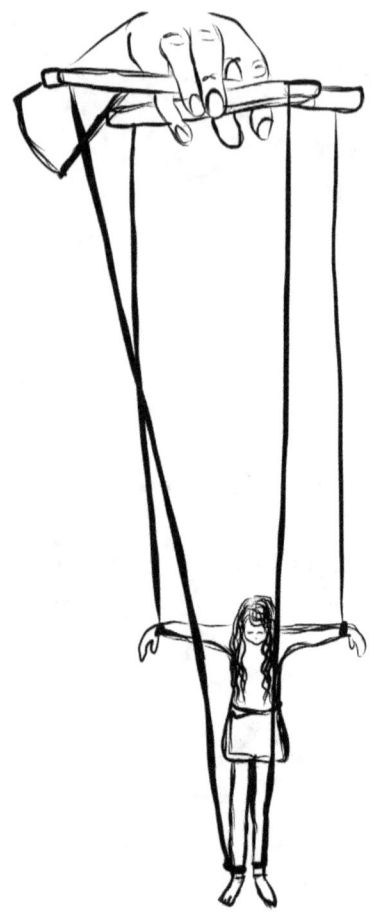

**Played**

You hated the idea of me being with someone else,
you chained me to your selfishness
and threw away the key.

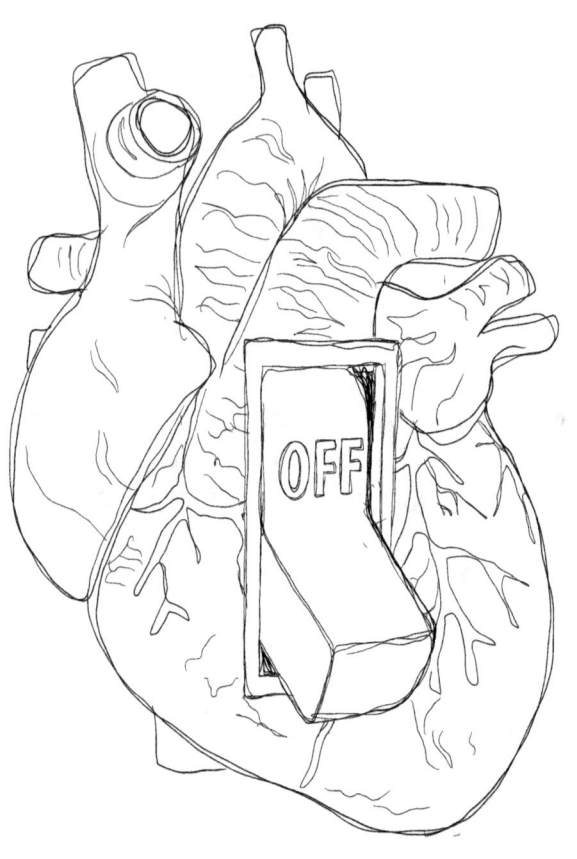

*Heartless*

**Replaced**

I forgot that I loved you,
there was someone better
filling in your place.

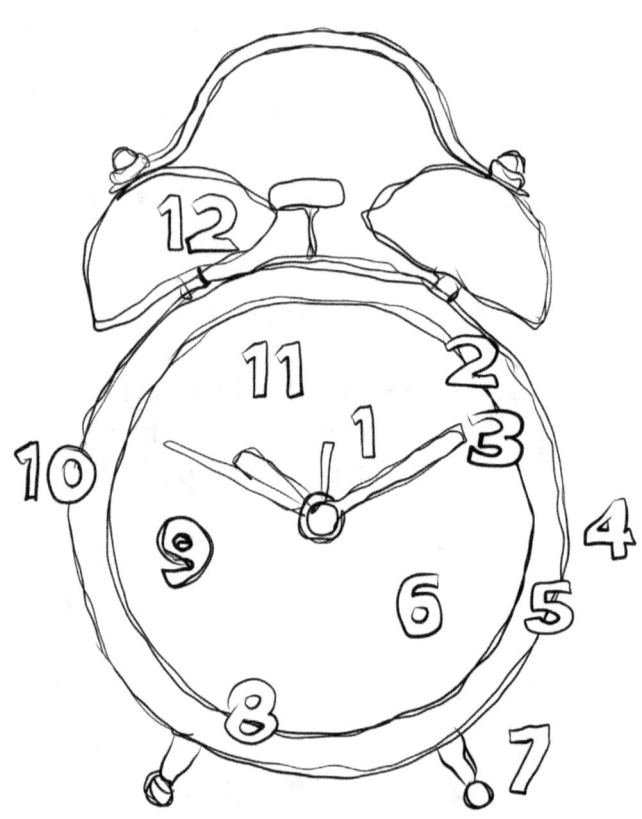

**Sweet Nightmare**

I dream of you

    and I intertwined

in the arms

    of happiness,

then I wake up.

**Unapologetic**

I apologize for being a handful of poems
you weren't interested to read.

I apologize for being a walking metaphor
you couldn't understand.

I apologize for being a run-on sentence
you couldn't keep up with.

I apologize for being what you wanted too soon
and what I needed too late.

## Metamorphosis

I wrote you a poem and
in the best way I could,
I tried to describe the butterflies you gave me.

They are now helplessly sheltered in cocoons.

**Contentment**

I am tired of being someone else's
missing piece. For once, I want
to complete myself.

**Tools**

We become careless and
begin to use people
to find you.

*Happiness*

**Infidelities**

She has visited the places
that know you best.

She has taken up space
in an area that consumes
most of your time.

She has been present
in moments and memories
that I never will,
but she will never make
them hers.

She will never make you
go back and whisper
her name.

She will never be me!

I may not have visited
places that know you best
or that see you when I can't,
but these spaces know me,
and wherever she goes,
she will hear my name.

### Residue

She follows footsteps
that lead to your heart,
only to find traces of me.

**Infatuated**

It's okay, baby, you can use me as your
parachute.
I'll be there to protect you
when you fall.

## Falling In Love With Me Is Hard

Fall in love with me.
Nobody ever
makes it out,
at least not as a
complete person.
I'm not saying
I would destroy you,
but I would take
a piece of you
and never give it back.
Fall in love with me.
I'll kidnap your emotions
and rename them after me
so that every time
you're with her,
and she asks you
to describe what loving
her feels like,
you'll be forced
to explain me.

## Routine

I practiced my goodbyes.
I wanted to be prepared this time.

## Ice Pack

My cold heart
compressed
against yours.

**Cleansed**

I wish I could remove
you out of my life
as the waves
erased our names
written in the sand.

The salt in the water
knew before me
that you were toxic,
and got rid of the dirt
in between my toes.

I don't want to bring you home,
we don't belong.

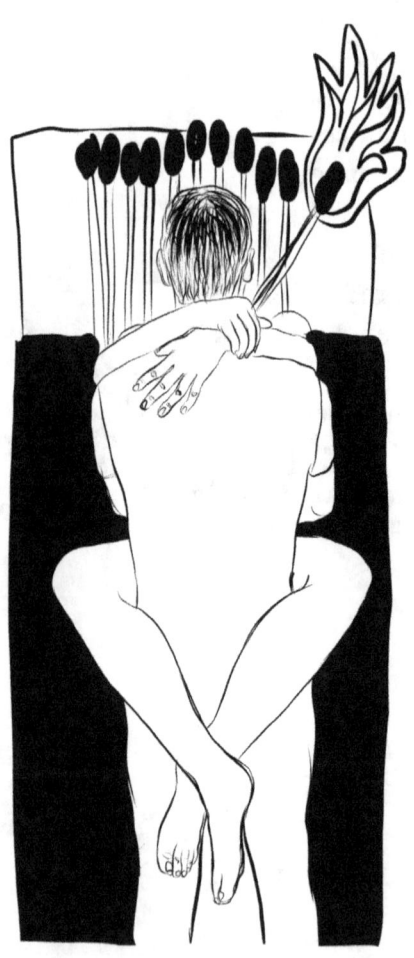

## The Fire Within

Do you know how much you hurt me?
You hurt me to the point,
I made fire
when I saw you.

**Cohesion**

I want to feel
what it feels
to kiss the lips
of consistency.

## Venom

I tried to fix you,
I tried to make you sweet again.
I tried helping you reconstruct your beehive.
I wanted to heal you, and you left
me full of bee stings, nothing else.

**Distraught**

Don't make me fall for you
when you're preoccupied
loving *someone else.*

*Heartful*

**Tinted**

The problem is
that we always want
to change someone.
We want to leave imprints
and tint memories
in as many places as possible
so that they remember us
if anything goes wrong.

Every time they visit those places,
our faces would be replicated
in every corner.
No matter the years,
these places will call your name.
The problem is that we matter,
and we believe we do,
but we just want others to feel it too.

**Bare**

I just want to lay next to you
with our clothes on,
but naked.

**Caress Me**

I like the way your lips touch
when you say my name.

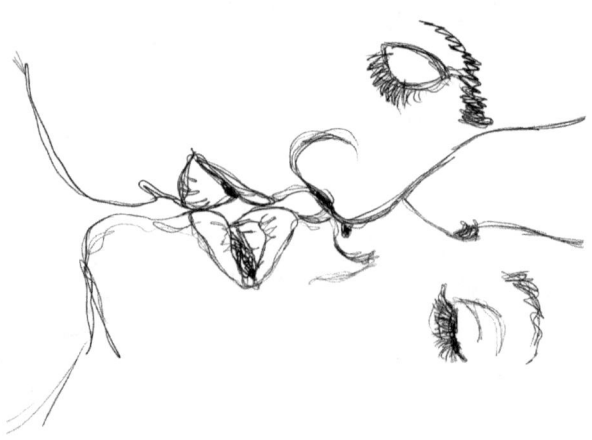

**Love Language**

Breathless,
you leave me breathless.
The kind of *breath*
that turns deserts
into strong ocean waves.
The type of *breath* that rests
on my neck when we're alone.
The kind of *breath* that
escapes your body
when my hands caress you.
That last *breath* you take
before I take your *breath* away.
The *breath* you take
a moment to listen to,
before making my
body your home.

That kind of *breath*.

**Reason to Live**

Poetry
is
your inside
screaming to be heard.
*Are you listening?*

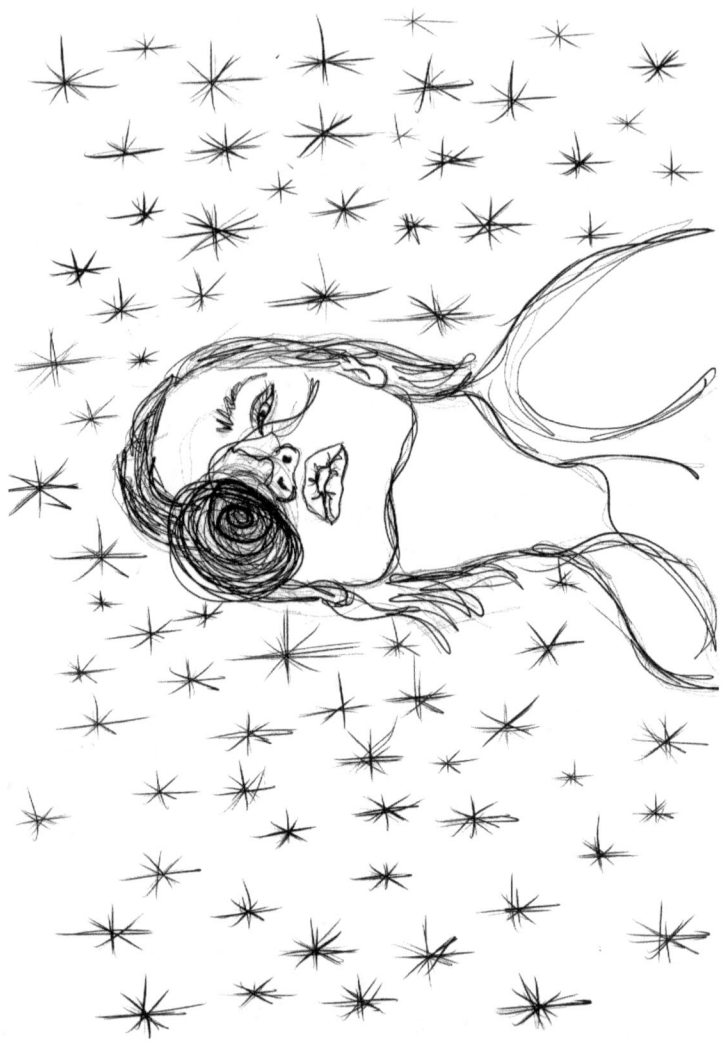

**The Place Where Time Slows**

Take me to that place
where my lips can brush yours
and paint canvases,
make poetry with your tongue
and music with your touch.

**Sweet Memories**

I stick post-it notes
on the memories
of you telling me
I looked beautiful.

**Oblivious**

I wonder what you think of me
when no one's around.

**Reminiscing**

When I hugged you for the first time,
I couldn't stop fighting with the idea
that this exact moment
will never happen again.

## The Storm

You can't
calm me,
much less
hold me back.

## Bliss

You will search for ways
to capture happiness
and store it in bottles
trapped in bodies
that will pop
and spray like
champagne.

## Happy



Your lips feel

**Hour**


                                    like Fridays.

**Undressed**

I've peeled myself to the skin
so that I could stand here naked
with you.

**Bonfire**

The truth
burns so much,
it can make a
campfire
in your heart
and melt your
emotions
like smores,
leaving you soft
and vulnerable
in a pile of ashes,
savoring
the chocolate
while ignoring the
burnt pieces of
marshmallow
in your mouth.

**The Art of Life**

When life gives you lemons, you make lemonade.
What do you do when life gives you scraps?
What do you make when life gives you broken
pieces and fragments of other fragile souls?
I know. You take those pieces and exchange them
for yours. And when they run out you realize
you've completed someone else's puzzle.
You watch them be missing pieces to someone
else, only to be left with just that, pieces.

What do you make then?
I know,
*you make poetry.*

## Apology Letter To Myself

I forgot
how powerful you can be,
and that was my biggest mistake.

**Remember To Water The Leaves**

Whatever you are looking for
is blinded by your negativity.
Let it all go, and it will find you.

**Touch**

I sometimes think I've lost my touch to move people without the need to use words, but my voice.

I sometimes think that poetry isn't for me anymore and that words are sometimes just that, words.

I sometimes think that art isn't art unless a paintbrush is involved and that pictures aren't worth a thousand words.

I sometimes think that poetic lines can't touch another soul deeper than mine.

I sometimes think of my writing caressing your back, touching you with minimal effort,
not reaching for you, but still reaching.

I have realized I still have my touch.

**Purpose**

I write for you,
for the masks we peel off
for one another
and scrape our love
out with forks.

I write for the
complicated and for the
unexplainable moments.
I write because
it's the only way
I learned to speak.
I write for me,
for those I love
and those I've lost.

I write because pain is art.

### Pieces of a Writer

My heart has been shattered to pieces
so that I can share them all with you.

*Thank you*

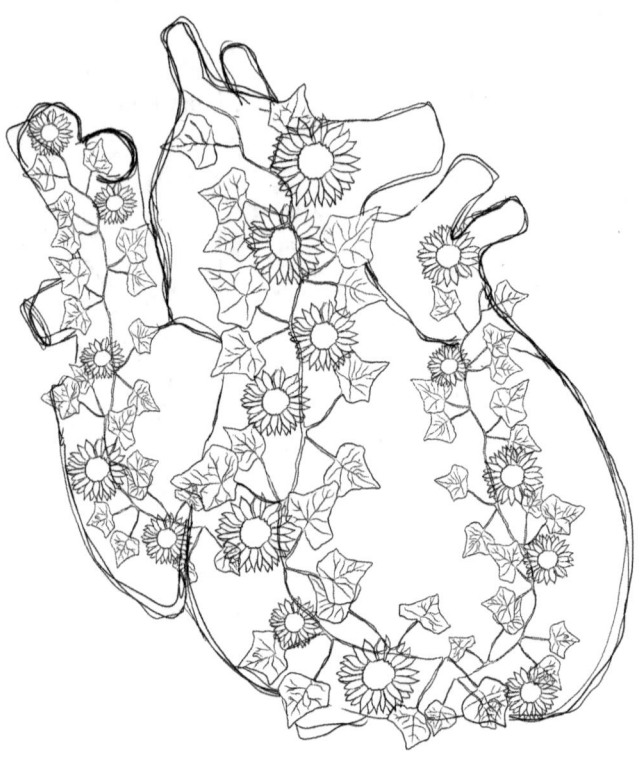

## A Hand Full

It's the courage to paste my heart
onto pages of a book,
hoping it reaches you.
A handful of rawness.
A handful of love.
A hand filled with poems.

# Acknowledgments

Thanks to my amazing husband for staying patient and understanding, and pushing me to follow my dreams. You showed me that being a poet is a poem itself, that a poem is more than words on paper, that poetry is who I am and that a great poem always takes time.

Edineida Martinez, you will always hold a special place in my heart. You are indeed the definition of a friend. You never let me give up, no matter how close I get to letting go. Thanks for always being just a call away.

Angy Abreu, thanks for turning me into the writer I am and for the writer I will be. You showed me that mistakes don't always turn out to have adverse outcomes. You welcomed me into a community full of support and love. I will always be thankful for you. You are indeed a gift from above. Thank you for seeing me.

Dominican Writers Association, thank you for being the community I needed. The community so many of us need. I know the organization will continue to grow and impact other writers the way you've impacted me. You are all amazing, and I will cherish you all forever.

Peggy Robles-Alvarado, you've changed me forever. You've pushed me to face my fears in ways I never thought possible. I admire you, and from the top, middle, & bottom of my heart. Thanks for everything.

Roxana Calderón, besides all my self-doubt, you are a perfect example of the poet I aim to be; never ashamed of pasting your heart onto the pages of a book for the world to see.

Dhayana Alejandrina, thank you for being a fantastic leader and inspiration. You are always willing to teach and uplift me. I've learned so much from you.

Carolina Abreu, thanks for your time and encouragement during the birth of my book.

To all my friends, family, and readers, thank you for inspiring me; my heart belongs to all of you.

Lastly, thanks to my past heartaches, heartbreaks, and heart-filling relationships. I couldn't have written this book without you.

## About The Author

**Massiel Alfonso** is a Dominican writer, author, poet, born and raised in Uptown, Manhattan. Massiel began writing poetry at the age of eleven. Her poetry explores topics such as love, heartbreak, trauma, loss and self-love. Through her poetry, Massiel looks to inspire those whose voices have been silenced and encourage others to share their story. She writes to find her voice and to inspire you to find yours. *Handful of Poems* is her first collection of poems, in her book she uncovers the aftermath of a broken heart and toxic relationships she's encountered throughout her young adult life. This book was written as a goodbye to all past relationships.

Her work has been published in Poetry Undressed (In The Dark, July 2021), La Libreta (No soy gringa, August 2021), Elle Leva Magazine (Soul Sex, September 2021), Spanglish Voces (Brugal Añejo, October 2021), and in She Rose Magazine (My Body Tells Me, December 2021).

Massiel is also a member of the Dominican Writers Association Writers Salon, lives in New Jersey and works as a Bilingual Elementary School Teacher.

www.ingramcontent.com/pod-product-compliance
Lightning Source LLC
Chambersburg PA
CBHW072058110526
44590CB00018B/3223